Find
Happiness
in Everything
You Do

Other books by

Susan Polis Schutz

Come Into the Mountains, Dear Friend
I Want to Laugh, I Want to Cry
Peace Flows from the Sky
Someone Else to Love
I'm Not That Kind of Girl
Yours If You Ask
Love, Live & Share

Find Happiness in Everything You Do

A collection of poems on friendship, love, family, careers and women's independence

Susan Polis Schutz

Designed and illustrated by
Stephen Schutz

Blue Mountain Press ™

Boulder, Colorado

Library of Congress Number: 81-71650
ISBN: 0-88396-177-6

Manufactured in the United States of America
First Printing: September, 1982

The following works have appeared previously in
Blue Mountain Arts publications:

"We had a beautiful little girl," and "Jordanna's long hair
blows." Copyright © Stephen Schutz and Susan Polis Schutz,
1980. "You are," "My Parents," "To My Mother," "I've been
wanting," "You are always," and "It takes more than
words." Copyright © Stephen Schutz and Susan Polis Schutz,
1981. All rights reserved.

Blue Mountain Press INC.

P.O. Box 4549, Boulder, Colorado 80306

CONTENTS

INTRODUCTION

During the past two years since writing LOVE, LIVE AND SHARE, I have been more at peace than in my whole life. I had a beautiful baby girl in July. I wrote poems about many of the feelings I had during this time: poems to Stephen about our ever-growing, exciting relationship; about my friends whom I don't often see; about my wonderful family; about my career; about older people who, I wish, were more honored in our society; and about women's independence. Many of these poems are published in this book.

I am still writing my autobiography, as well as another non-fiction book. I continue to love Stephen more than ever. We hibernate in our home, or outside in nature, so that we can be with our two children every minute when we are not working. The strength and love of a close family unit is constantly proving to be my most important source of happiness. I am able to be more creative, accomplish more in my career, be more sensitive to things, understand more and be more appreciative of life, with my family at my side.

We now have publishers in over thirty-five countries: from Sweden to Singapore — from Jamaica to Japan; and our works have been translated into Spanish, German and Hebrew. It is extremely gratifying to find that people in foreign countries relate to our poetry and art as they do in America. It proves that all people, no matter where they come from, have the same feelings and emotions. There need not be war. There need not be nuclear weapons. If only people would rule countries with concern and friendship, rather than fear and deceit, the world would live in peace and love.

Thank you for listening to my thoughts — FIND HAPPINESS IN EVERYTHING YOU DO.

Susan Polis Schutz

April, 1982

Find
Happiness
in Friendship

Though we don't see each other very much
nor do we write to each other very much
nor do we phone each other very much
I always know that, at any time,
I could call, write or see you
and everything would be exactly the same
You would understand everything I am saying
and everything that I am thinking

Our friendship does not depend
on being together
It is deeper than that
Our closeness is something inside of us
that is always there
ready to be shared with each other
whenever the need arises

It is such a comfortable and warm feeling
to know that
we have such a lifetime
friendship

You are always my friend
when I am happy
or when I am sad
when I am all alone
or when I am with people
You are always my friend
if I see you today
or if I see you a year from now
if I talk to you today
or if I talk to you a year from now
You are always my friend
and though through the years
we will change
It doesn't matter what I do
or it doesn't matter what you do
Throughout our lifetime
you are always my friend

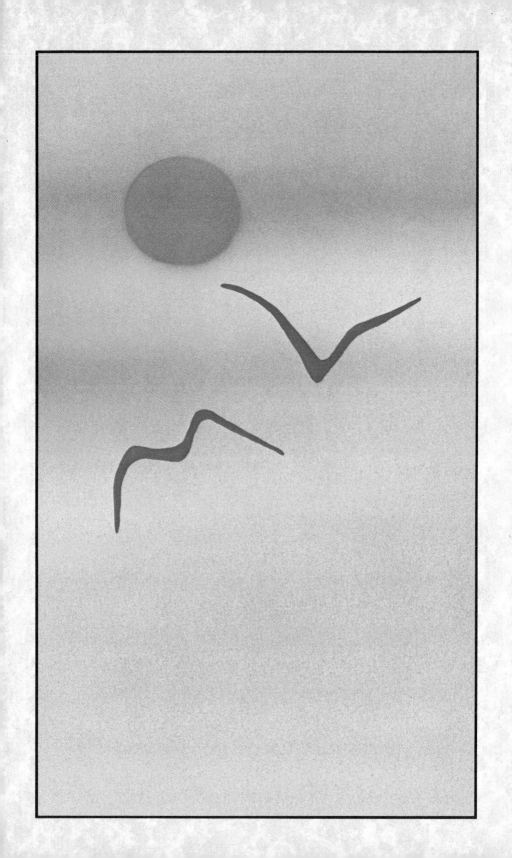

Regardless of
whom I meet
or what I do
or what I have become
it is the friends
I grew up with
that I feel
closest to
and that I have
the most in common with
Though we don't see
each other often
when we do
it is as though
we were always together —
so comfortable
so natural
so honest
I guess old friends
who know where we come from
who know our backgrounds
who know our families
have an understanding
of us
that no new friend
can ever have

When you need someone
to talk to
talk to me
When you need someone
to laugh with
laugh with me
When you need someone
to advise you
turn to me
When you need someone
to help you
let me help you
Understanding each other's
individual needs
and calling upon each other
in good and bad times
is what a real friendship is
I thank you deeply
for providing
such a friendship

It takes more than words
to let you know
how much it means to me
to have you as a friend
I can depend on you for understanding
when I am confused
I can depend on you for comfort
when I am sad
I can depend on you for laughter
when I am happy
I am so thankful
to know that you are
always
my friend

You are always
so understanding
You are always
so concerned
You are always
so caring
You are always
so giving
You are always
so helpful
But most important
you are always
my friend

I miss your thoughts
I miss your words
I miss your actions
but knowing that we
     share our feelings
even though apart
it is as though
you were with me now

Since we live
so far from each other
we must try
extra hard
to keep in touch with each other
I wish you would write
or call more often
but I know that you
get so involved
with everyday events
that there's never enough time
I forgive you for this
because I know that I am
in your thoughts as you
are in mine
I hope that
my friendship with you
is as important
as your friendship
is to me

When I sit down
and think about what is
important to me
I always think of you
and I am so
appreciative of
our closeness
our understanding of each other
and our friendship

Though we have
    changed somewhat —
    doing different things
    living in different places
    living with different life-styles —
our backgrounds can
never change
Since we were friends
when we were growing up
our closeness can
never change
and I now know
that our friendship
will last
forever

You have such a
positive outlook on life
Your words are always encouraging
Your face is lit up with excitement
Your actions are so straightforward
Your inner strength helps you achieve so much
When people are around you
they seem to absorb your uplifting attitude
When I think about you
I can only think
of happiness
and how lucky I am
to know
you

Today I woke up
     and thought about you
     I went to work
     and thought about you
     I went to lunch
and thought about you
I went home at night
and thought about you
You are
always in my thoughts
and even though we are not together
you are a very important
part of my days

I know that
     I acted silly
and did things
     I am now very
sorry about
I didn't know what to do
when you hurt me
so I reacted impulsively
with the quickest way to
hurt you back
It is unbelievable what
emotions can make
a usually stable person do
In the future I am going
to try my hardest
to discuss any problems
that might occur
or tell you if you
hurt me
rather than
lashing viciously and fiercely back
at you
I like you far too much
to hurt you
Please forgive me

I've been wanting
to write to you
but I have been
sort of afraid to
It's been so
long since we have
seen or heard from
each other
but I think of
you and all the
things we used
to do together
I remember the kind of
understanding and closeness
that we had
Let's forget
about the times that
we missed together
I would love
to resume
our friendship once
again

Find Happiness in Your Family

To My Mother

For as long as I can remember
you were always by my side
to give me support
to give me confidence
to give me help

For as long as I can remember
you were always the person I looked up to
so strong
so sensitive
so pretty

For as long as I can remember
and still today
you are everything
a mother should be

For as long as I can remember
you always provided stability within our family
full of laughter
full of tears
full of love

Whatever I have become
is because of you
and I thank you
forever
for our
relationship

To My Parents, Thank You

You were always there
to help me
You were always there
to guide me
You were always there
to laugh with me
You were always there
to cry with me
But most important
You were always
there to love me
And believe me
I am always
here to love you

What more beautiful sight
is there than for
you to run along the beach
with our angelic little son following
and his little puppy following him
You run in and out of the waves
playing and laughing, chasing after each other

I sit in the sand
on the chair you both made for me
to make me more comfortable
seven more weeks before we have our new baby

I am so happy
to have such a beautiful family
so happy to be so much in love
I have dedicated my whole life
to being with you
every minute of the day and night
and to loving you and our son
every minute of the day and night

She came off the
sight-seeing helicopter
and ran into her son's arms
Her smile shared the
beauty that she had seen
with her son
Her son, in turn, hugged
the baby
Another mother threw
a small snowball at her daughter
The daughter ducked and
the mother and daughter hugged
each other after the game
laughing together about how
bad their aim was
And they ran
into the warm house
to tell the rest of the family
about their fun
The father picked up
his baby daughter and
she grinned with love
He put his head to hers
and the baby kissed him
These are moments
which matter
which feel
and which are
so important in life
The love between a family and
the moments spent together
are the only answers
to all that is
so crazy in the world

The three of you
    your blue eyes
        sparkling
        your inner beauty

The three of you
your skin radiating
your freshness

The three of you
your expressions showing
your sense of humor

The three of you
your color showing
your fragileness

The three of you
your lips
laughing your humor

The three of you
your beings are
my life

We had a beautiful little girl
I want to shout it to the clouds
I want to yell it across the ocean
It's all over

We had a beautiful little girl
Nine months of worry
            and discomfort
and there she was
all pink and cuddly
with long almond-shaped eyes
perfect little hands and feet

We had a beautiful little girl
I want to shout it across the mountains
I want to yell it through the fields
It's all over

Jordanna is beautiful
Jordanna is healthy
Jordanna is perfect
Thank you Jordanna
Thank you God

Across
        the street
     a man stands
        hugging a
           little baby

in his arms
so gently and
so sensitively

It is
so beautiful and
so touching
to see a strong man
openly loving his baby
especially when that
man is your husband
and you are
the mother of the baby

I could rock you
  in my arms forever
I could look into
  your button eyes forever
I could play with
  your little fingers forever
I could watch your adorable grin forever
I will love you forever
my beautiful little baby

My little baby
I had to leave you
for several days
I keep seeing your
bright eyes laughing
with mine
I feel your soft cheeks
against mine
I hear your soft coos
In only two months
you have become so much
an individual life
so much a real part of my life
I promise never
to leave you again
You have become so
much a part
of me

Jordanna's long hair blows in the wind
　　She is a symbol of freedom
　　Jordanna's lips pucker shut
　　　　when she doesn't want food
　　She is a symbol of determination
Jordanna is a woman of the world,
a Keller woman of strength
Jordanna is a baby of love,
a baby of beauty
Jordanna is ours
Jordanna is yours

Mommy, pick me up please
Mommy, help me
I'm hungry
The food is hot
I'm tired
That is pretty
That is nice
That is mine
The depth of feeling and
expression that you have
at one and a half years old
is miraculous
Every day you learn a new word
Every day you learn a new emotion
The people around you must be so
careful and sensitive
to how things affect you
because everything we do
is picked up and copied by you
and how we feel and act
is understood by you
and will remain inside you
forever

My little angel
Why do you cry
Where does it hurt
I will make it better

My little angel
Why are you laughing
What is so funny
Let me continue your happiness

My little angel
Your eyes are so big
Your smile is so beautiful
I hold you close
and feel your comfort
Let me always be here
for you
in every way possible
to help you have
a perfect life

You sit and play
so contentedly
with your toys
Every once in a while
you stand up, smile,
and dance to
my record
I look at you
your innocence
your laughter
your happiness
your simplicity
your beauty
and I wonder
where you
will be
in fifteen years
and I wonder
where the world
will be
in fifteen years
I just hope
that you will
be able to
enjoy a life of
sensitivity
goodness
accomplishment
happiness
and love
in a world
that is
at
peace

My little angel
I sit and hold you
while you rest in my arms
I can't stop smiling at you
and you always smile back
I kiss your forehead softly
You look at me with love
You say, "Mommy"
I say, "Baby"
You say, "Mommy"
I say, "Baby"
You smile so sweetly
and fall asleep
I kiss your forehead
and hug you so tightly
that you're sure of my vast love
even while you're sleeping
You're such a
beautiful
good
sweet
baby
I could rock you
in my arms
forever and ever

My little boy
now that you are
able to read
you might read
this book and
wonder why there
are so many poems
to your sister
Do I love her more?
Of course not, honey
It was such a beautiful experience
having you and your sister
Since I express my feelings best
by writing them down
I wrote a whole book about you
when you were born
And now that your sister is born
I write poems about her
So read the poems, and continue
my little boy
to share with us
our love and
excitement
of your little sister

My little boy
thank you
for being so
kind and so
gentle and so
sensitive with
your new sister
It is beautiful
the way you look at her
with love
She is very lucky
to have
you as
her brother
and as her very
favorite
person

My Son

From the day you
were born
you were
so special
so smart
so sensitive
so good
It was so much fun
to watch you
As you grew
you became your
own person
with your own
ideas
and your own way
of doing things
It was so exciting
to watch you
As you grew more
you became more independent
still special
still smart
still sensitive
still good
I am so proud
of everything about you
and I want you to know
that I love
everything about you

My son
looked at
me with
his large
blue eyes
and said,
"Mommy,
please don't
finish your
life story."
I asked
him why.
He didn't
want to
tell me.
Finally
he put
his mouth
to my ear
and whispered
"If you
write about your
life
it sounds
as if
you are
old."
I explained
to him
that I'm
only writing
about
when I
was twenty
until twenty-eight.
He said,
"Well, okay,
but I still
don't want
you to finish
it."

"Why not, honey?"
"Well if you
do, you'll
be more famous
and the phone
will ring more
and it will even
ring all the time
on the week-ends
and then you'll
have to talk
to everyone in
the streets
and we'll have
to go to all
the cities
and you'll
have to go
on all those TV shows
and everyone will
say, 'Oh, Susan'
and you'll
have to talk
to everyone
and you will be
a big shot
and everyone
will keep
talking to you."
I said,
"Well, what's
wrong with
all that?"
His eyes got
bigger and he
said softly,
"Well, then
you won't
have time
for me."

Honey
You want a
mother who is
not only very
happy with
her family
but is also happy
with herself
Well, each woman
is different
Some Mommies
stay home and take
care of their house
Other Mommies
work at other kinds of jobs
I am, as you know, a writer
My work is very important to me
Daddy's work is very important to him
What happens with our work
is very important to us
But always remember this,
nothing, absolutely nothing
is as important to us
as you

Thank you for the fun we have
Thank you for the understanding we have
Thank you for the respect we have
Thank you for the truth we have
Thank you for the values we share
Thank you for the beauty we share
Thank you for the happiness we share
Thank you for the love we share
Thank you for the life we share
Thank you for
being my
family

To the Parents of the Man I Love

You did a wonderful
job of raising your
son
He is so kind
and so sensitive
and so good
By being his parents
you set examples and
values which
he upholds and stands for
today
You taught him
that there should be
no preconceived roles
for men and women
and that is why
we have such an equal
relationship
You taught him
to be honest
forthright
and strong
I thank you for
being such great parents
to the man
I love

My Parents

You are
   so loving
   so giving
   so caring
   so special —
I thank God
that I was
born
to
you

Find
Happiness
in Everything
You Do

She was a famous doctor
        Her patient was waiting in the room
        As she answered an important phone call
        I heard her say
        "No, you take the blue car
        your brother needs the white one.
No you can't, your brother
is going on a trip this weekend
and the white car is more dependable.
No I can't lend you mine.
Use the blue car, okay?"
She hung up the phone
and quickly went inside to
her patients
I laughed out loud
picturing a man of
equal career status
getting such a phone call
before a board of directors' meeting
Of course he would not
get such a call
because the family wouldn't bother him
at work
No matter what
type of work
a woman does
she is still the one
who solves the
children's problems
who plans what they will and will not do
and who organizes each member of the family
all while living up to
the demands of her own work
Women need to be so much
more versatile than men
to exist
successfully
in this world

We cannot
listen to what
others want us
to do
We must listen
to ourselves
Society
family
friends
do not know what
we must do
Only we know
and only we
can do what is
right for us
So start
right now
You will need to
work very hard
You will need to
overcome many obstacles
You will need to go
against the better
judgment of many people
and you will need to
bypass their prejudices
But you can have
whatever you want
if you
try hard
enough
So start right now and
you will live
a life designed
by you and
for you
and you will
love
your
life

A woman will get only what she seeks
You must choose your goals carefully
Know what you like
and what you do not like
Be critical about what you can do well
and what you cannot do well
Choose a career or lifestyle that interests you
and work hard to make it a success
Enter a relationship that is worthy of
everything you are physically and mentally capable of
Be honest with people, help them if you can
but don't depend on anyone to make life easy
or happy for you
Only you can do that for yourself
Strive to achieve all that you like
Find happiness in everything you do
Love with your entire being
Make a triumph
of every aspect
of your life

 **M**ore than ever
I am able
to appreciate
the awesomeness
of the mountains
the roaring of the waves
the purple of the wildflowers
the magnificence of nature
now that
you are a
part of my
life

"**I**'m terribly sorry.
I can't be on your show.
My daughter has an earache."
"You what?"
"I can't be on your show.
My daughter has an earache."
"Are you crazy?
No one cancels this show."
"I'm really sorry but
she can't fly now."
"Well why can't you?"
"Because I can't leave her."
"Are you crazy?"
"I'm sorry. If I
had had more notice
I would have been in New York City now
and there wouldn't have been a problem."
"Do you realize that this is the biggest show on TV?"
"Yes I do and I'd love to be on it, but I can't right now."
"I don't know who
you think you are."
"I'm really sorry. You'll have no
trouble replacing me."
"You're damn right. I can list 1,000 people
who will come with three-minutes' notice.
I'll always remember this. Your
daughter has an earache so
you can't be on my TV show.
Sure—okay. Are you positive?"
"Yes I am. I can't leave my daughter."
"Is she very sick?"
"No, but she can't go on a plane now."
"I think you're crazy. This is a first."

Older people
could teach us
so much
if we would
only listen
Their wisdom
their simplicity
their experiences
their many years of living
We need them to
live with us
with our families
to teach us
and our children
all they know
to love us
and to let us
love them
and to let us
help them
when they
need it
A family
is not complete
without its
eldest
members

The Kings and Queens of Our Families

Old people's skin
   is not as soft as a baby's
   because they have worked
      for such a long time
   Their eyes
   are not as innocent as a baby's eyes
because they have seen so much more
Their minds
are not as clear as a baby's
because of all the clutter of the years gone by
But in many ways
they are like babies
Natural and beautiful
they need extra love and help
to survive
But in this society
rather than have one family
love and care for them
they are sent away
to a home
like a child would be
sent to an orphanage
This is a hideous
thing to do to people
who help us grow up
who are responsible for our
being here
who were once
everything we are
Older people should be
the most respected
members of our
society
They should share
in any of our
happiness and
all of our caring
They should be
the kings and queens
of our
families

Find Happiness in Love

Love is
    being happy for the other person
        when they are happy
    being sad for the person
        when they are sad
  being together in good times
  and being together in bad times
Love is the source of strength

Love is
    being honest with yourself at all times
    being honest with the other person at all times
    telling, listening, respecting the truth,
    and never pretending
Love is the source of reality

Love is
    an understanding so complete that
    you feel as if you are a part of the other person
    accepting the other person just the way they are
    and not trying to change them to be something else
Love is the source of unity

Love is
    the freedom to pursue your own desires
    while sharing your experiences with the other person
    the growth of one individual alongside of
    and together with the growth of another individual
Love is the source of success

Love is
    the excitement of planning things together
    the excitement of doing things together
Love is the source of the future

Love is
    the fury of the storm
    the calm in the rainbow
Love is the source of passion

Love is
    giving and taking in a daily situation
    being patient with each other's needs and desires
Love is the source of sharing

Love is
    knowing that the other person
    will always be with you regardless of what happens
    missing the other person when they are away
    but remaining near in heart at all times
Love is the source of security

Love is
 the
source
 of
life

You are
  so kind
  so gentle
  so caring
You are
  so confident in yourself that
you are not afraid to show
  a strong sensitivity
  a strong vulnerability
  a strong beauty
To be so in touch
with your feelings
and emotions
is very important to me
and very important
in having a successful relationship

I want to thank you
for being such
a great person

Everything I feel and
everything I want to feel
involves you
Everything I do and
everything I want to do
is with you
Everything I say and
everything I want to say
is to you
Everything I love and
everything I want to love
is you

When I see you happy
I too am happy
When I see you sad
I too am sad
When I see you not feeling well
I too do not feel well
When I see you full of energy
I too am full of energy
It always amazes me that
though we are two different people
independent in both thought and action
I feel and act the way you do
I guess your moods and feelings
affect me so greatly because
I love you
and I feel so much
a part of you

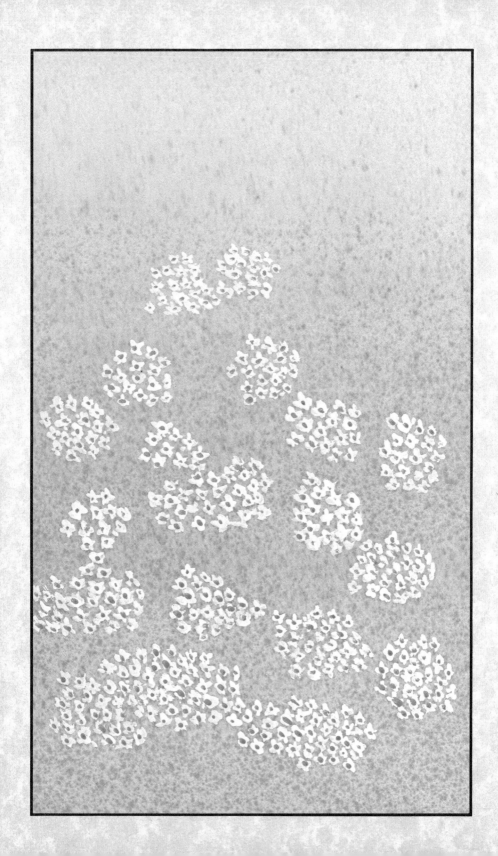

Sometimes I get so scared
that something will happen to you
Tears begin to flow uncontrollably
I guess this is the way my mind
emphasizes how very vital you are to me
I must make every minute
spent with you important
and I must always
let you know and feel
all the time
how much
I love you

I want to
have a relationship with you that
is free
from all societal pressures
I want to
have a relationship with you that
is honest
about every aspect of life
I want to
have a relationship with you
that is strong
regardless of what is happening
I want to
have a relationship with you
that is exciting
every day and night
I want a relationship
that grows with age
that thrives on love
and that is the most
important part of our lives
forever

You always believe
that anything is possible
All we have to do
is say we need something
and you will make it happen
even if we think it is impossible
Your confident attitude of
sense and accomplishment
teaches people around you
to try harder
You set such a
good example for the
children
They copy you
because they love you
and they too
feel as though
they can accomplish anything
Thank you for
being such an inspiration
to all of
us

pink and pastel yellow

pink pink and pastel yellow pastel yellow

dark pink dark pink and yellow yellow

Blue Blue pink Blue Blue Blue

Blue Blue Blue Blue Blue Blue

Blue Red Purple Blue Red Purple Blue Red Purple Blue Red Purple

Black Red Blue Purple Black Red Blue Purple Black

Black Red Blue Purple Black Red Blue Purple Black

Black Red Black Red Purple Black Red Black Red Purple Black

RED RED RED BLACK PURPLE RED RED RED RED

RED RED RED BLACK PURPLE RED RED RED RED

RED RED RED RED RED RED RED RED PURPLE RED RED

RED RED RED RED RED RED RED RED RED RED RED

RED RED RED RED RED RED RED RED RED RED RED RED

RED BLACK PURPLE RED RED BLACK PURPLE RED

RED BLACK RED BLACK

dark pink dark pink and yellow yellow

pink pink and pastel yellow pastel yellow

pink and pastel yellow

Many of the things that
you do are
so thoughtful and
so kind and
so loving and
so sensitive
I thank you deeply for these things

Some of the things that
you do are
so careless and
so thoughtless and
so gruff
I thank you for these things too
because they show me that
you are not perfect
and I am reminded
that neither am I
And by admitting this
our expectations for each other
will not be too great to bear
Our relationship will not be a
fantasy with disappointment
but it will be
a reality full of
joy

I dislike so much
the times when
I am angry at you
or when you are
angry at me
We need to
talk about our feelings more
and not harbor resentment
We need to
immediately tell each other
why we feel hurt or mad
so we can make amends
Our days are too short
to waste any time on
not being completely happy
with each other
I want to spend
every second of
every day and night
loving you
completely

When you are away
everything feels only half right
my mind cannot concentrate
on anything completely
When I work I only half work
When I play I only half play
When I sleep I only half sleep
When I think I only half think
because the other half of my mind
is always
with
you

You are so special
so honest
so sensitive
so sincere
You are so unique
so individualistic
so creative
so beautiful
Thank you
for being the most wonderful person
I have ever known

The mountains create huge
     walls around the earth
    The forests cast tall shadows
      in the sky
    The oceans fill the land
  with an echo
The flowers color the ground with beauty
In this huge, vast world
I feel so very lucky
to be able to
find someone
whom I want to
share all my thoughts with
and all my activities with
In this huge, vast world
I feel so very lucky
to be able to find
someone
I love
Thank you

With you
  I am able to
    be myself
  I am able to
    be honest
I am able to have freedom
I am able to make mistakes
With you
I am able to share my thoughts
I am able to share my love
I am able to share my life

When things are confused
I discuss them with you
until they make sense

When something good happens
you are the first person I tell
so I can share my happiness

When I don't know what to do in a situation
I ask your opinion
and weigh it heavily with mine

When I am lonely
I call you
because I never feel alone with you

When I have a problem
I ask for your help
because your wiseness helps me to solve it

When I want to have fun
I want to be with you
because we have such a great time together

When I want to talk to someone
I always talk to you
because you understand me

When I want the truth about something
I call you
because you are so honest

It is so essential
to have you in my life
Thank you for being my friend
Thank you for being my love

You can never disappoint me
because I know your strength
and I know your weaknesses
You can never disappoint me
because I know what you can do
and I know what you cannot do
You can never disappoint me
because I know that you are always honest with me
and I know that you are always honest with yourself
You can never disappoint me
because I love you
exactly the way
you are

After a long
        day's work
        or when I am very tired
            every little thing
        bothers me
and I will say or do things
which I do not mean
Please realize that my words
are not intended to hurt you
or to be mean
Please realize that
I am only expressing
the frustrations of my day
and since you are with me
at these times
you are the receiver
of my words
I am sorry if I hurt you
I love you
so much

We built a world together —
a world of fun
a world of creativity
a world of nature
a world of passion
We built a life together —
A life of honesty
A life of understanding
A life of freedom
A life of
love

Let me be the person
that you walk with in the mountains
Let me be the person
that you pick flowers with
Let me be the person
that you tell all your inner feelings to
Let me be the person
that you talk to in confidence
Let me be the person
that you turn to in sadness
Let me be the person
that you smile with in happiness
Let me be the person
that you
love

I am always here
to understand you
I am always here
to laugh with you
I am always here
to cry with you
I am always here
to talk with you
I am always here
to think with you
I am always here
to plan with you
Even though we
might not always
be together
please know that
I am always
here to
love
you

ABOUT THE AUTHORS

Susan Polis Schutz began writing at age seven, and to the delight of millions of readers, she has been writing ever since. She is the author of six best-selling books of poetry — Come Into the Mountains, Dear Friend; I Want to Laugh, I Want to Cry; Peace Flows from the Sky; Someone Else to Love; Yours If You Ask; and Love, Live and Share.

Susan grew up in a small country town, Peekskill, New York. She graduated from Rider College earning degrees in English and Biology. After attending graduate school in New York City, Susan taught elementary school and wrote articles for magazines and newspapers.

In 1965 she met Stephen Schutz. Stephen, a native New Yorker, studied at the New York High School of Music and Art where he practiced the basics of drawing and calligraphy. His great love and appreciation of art became overshadowed by physics books and lab tables at M.I.T. and Princeton University (where he received a Ph.D. Degree in Theoretical Physics in 1970), but it surfaced again when he moved to Colorado for post-graduate work.

Following his marriage to Susan in 1969 and his increasing love for his inspirational surroundings, Stephen decided to give up his career in physics. This decision allowed him to devote his time to the development and perfection of his artistic techniques, and it gave Stephen and Susan the opportunity to do what they most wanted to do . . . spend their time together.

In 1972 Come Into the Mountains, Dear Friend, Susan's first book of poems with Stephen's illustrations, was published. The public acceptance of this book was phenomenal, and history was made in the process. It became apparent that people readily identified with Susan's poetic words and Stephen's mystical illustrations, and by the end of that year, their joint career, combined with a very special love, became their way of life.

Susan and Stephen pursue creative paths which continually diverge and meet again. A variety of interests and concerns keep them involved in new and exciting things. In addition to designing and illustrating all of Susan's books, Stephen Schutz has artistically complemented the works of many other well-known authors. He has also created beautiful notecards, stationery and prints featuring his gentle airbrush blends, unique calligraphy and exceptional photography. A man of many interests, Stephen continues to study physics as a hobby and maintains his special rapport with the outdoors, manifested in his frequent hiking trips in the mountains, swimming in the ocean and cross-country skiing along the Continental Divide. Stephen is truly a very talented and ''self-contained'' man.

In addition to Susan's books of poetry, many of her poems have been published on notecards and prints and in magazines and text books, and she has edited books by other well-known authors. She is also writing an autobiographical novel and is co-authoring a book entitled **What Every Woman Should and Must Know About Her Body**, a project undertaken with the first woman doctor to head an obstetrics department of a major hospital. The conviction with which Susan expresses feminist ideas does not preclude an equally intense commitment to her family. Her efforts to weave together a modern female independence with the classical idea of love is a source of harmony in her work.

A special kind of talent is required to translate feelings into poems and emotions into paintings, and Susan and Stephen have that rare gift. It is a gift that has been shared with more than 300 million people around the world. Susan and Stephen's works have been translated into Spanish, German, Hebrew, and Afrikaans, and have been published in Great Britain, Republic of Ireland, Germany, Australia, Argentina, Pakistan, Nigeria, the Netherlands and Israel, and distributed in the rest of the nations of the world. In a time of constant fluctuation in social, religious and political standards, Susan and Stephen's expressions serve to remind us all of our inner spirit and our basic values. As a British newspaper recently commented, ''her modern freestyle poems matched by his artistry, touch the soul.''

Photo by Barry Staver

Photos by Barry Staver